For all who are searching…

PASSPORT FOR A NEW IDENTITY IN CHRIST

Mikaël REALE

© *2018 Mikaël REALE)*

Illustration: **Mare Nostrum Project**
© 2016 Mikaël REALE/VLED

Edition: BoD—Books on Demand
12/14 rond-point des Champs Elysées
75008 Paris FRANCE
Imprimé par BoD – Books on Demand, Norderstedt

ISBN: 9782322122899

Dépôt légal : **Juin 2018**

All right reserved for all country.
First Published in French by:
Vraiment Libre Edition 2008
ISBN: 2-915554-01-3

Where have you been, Son?

When writing a book, I like to start by describing my own experience. I believe that our experiences lend depth to what could be just dry theory. So, here is an experience that changed my life and my ministry, a few years ago.

To put this anecdote back into context, let me fill you in on the details of the situation.

In 1995, my family and I went to Madagascar to do missionary work. We planted a church over there, with meetings happening in our garage, which rapidly took form. God then gave us development strategies, which quickly bore fruit in abundance.

This brought us to a place whereby we were forming people and building up future leaders. God showed us couples that we were to concentrate on. For three years, we developed the churches, the social and humanitarian aspects, and established strong friendships with those who would one day take over from us. But I will tell you more of that later.

After three years, we had planted 4 churches, a Christian school, an orphanage, and formed a hundred or so leaders of different churches in the country. It was at that moment that, after two serious cases of malaria, we moved to the Reunion Island.

Our settling-in to this French-speaking island was marked by a miracle from God. Once again, we found ourselves starting a house church in our living room. Again, God gave us a strategy and the movement started gaining strength. After a few months, we opened a second, and then a third church on the island. In 18 months we had had over 200 baptisms.

The success of my ministry meant I was invited to help out in Mauritius. I went along every two months to assist young churches and form leaders. I was also regularly invited to France, England, Belgium and Israel.

I was writing my second book at the time, and had lots of projects: to open a missionary training center in the Reunion Island for French-speaking Christians, a Christian school, to make a CD with our worship group, etc. It seemed nothing could stop this outpouring "revival" we were experiencing.

And yet, in the space of a few weeks, following an

accidental death of a church member, and due to the undermining work of an ill-intentioned member of the leadership, I was forced to close one of the churches. Another church decided to leave the group of churches under my leadership. Our projects for the Christian School and missionary training had to be canceled. Vicious rumors about us started to circulate. The friends we had made in the ministry started to turn their backs on us, and people whom we had led to the Lord were no longer speaking to us…

Cathy, my wife, and I decided to take a year "out," a "sabbatical," and God opened a way for us in England.

With no support anymore, I had to find a job, and so landed up in a service station. I worked evenings from 6 pm 'till 11 pm. I spent the evenings swiping credit cards in the till.

After having had responsibilities in the Indian Ocean islands, this work seemed so degrading. I had passed from being a leader of an internationally recognized, successful group of churches, to being an immigrant worker.

It was a very testing time, and I found myself sliding into a depression. With the loss of my ministry, I had lost my reason for living. I no longer prayed, nor opened my bible, and only went to church for my children's sake.

This situation lasted for three months, until one evening God showed up at the petrol station where I was working.

There was nobody about, as a thin icy rain had driven even the bravest souls home early. Boredom gripped me, and I still had two hours before I could close up for the night. Having nothing to do, I started praying, more mechanically than consciously. It was as if my spirit, having been deprived of prayer, had made the most of the apathy of my soul to reconnect with God.

It didn't need much for the Lord to come to meet me. The atmosphere in the room changed, and before I could realize what was happening, God spoke to me out loud. *"Where have you been, Son?"*

If the fact that God spoke surprised me, the question made me angry. What did he mean "where had I been?" I had spent the last six years in the mission field, I had worn my family out, I nearly lost my life several times, I hadn't taken more than three weeks' holiday in six years, and not even one day off a week, and God was asking where I had been.

Even before I got to the end of my list, God's presence had disappeared.

That said, the fact that I could feel His presence, after months of sulking, made me start praying again.

God came back with the same question, and, alas, my reaction was the same. I couldn't stand the idea that all that work and the price I had paid, weren't recognized. I tried to fill my time at the station, tidying the shelves and cleaning my counter, but very soon I realized that I was missing something essential. I started to pray, and God came back, patiently, with the same question, but this time the Holy Spirit pointed out the key word of the question: SON!

Of course, God knew where I had been during these years. He had been there all the time, rejoicing at my success and lamenting at my failures. But something essential had been missing from our relation, I no longer came to him as a son!

The Holy Spirit reminded me of all the times I had prayed over the last few years. Each time it was to ask for something as finances for the church, anointing for my ministry, a good message to preach, solutions for problems, healing for people, etc.

Then God reminded me that years before that, I used to come into his presence just to be with him, praise and worship, to share a moment with him, as I loved him, he was my father, and I was his son.

The Holy Spirit told me: *"The Father gave his only son, to be reconciled with you, for you to be his son, not a member of his household staff.'*

In fact, this was the second time that God had told

me he missed me. The first time whilst I was preparing a convention in the Indian Ocean islands, God set me aside to talk to me as a father to a son. I spent three super days in his presence, but I hadn't grasped the fact that this should be more than just a once in a while things. Soon I was back to the non-stop action of my daily life.

So, God simply removed the obstacle from our relationship: my ministry!

This revelation lifted me from my depressive state immediately, and changed my "sabbatical year" into a "year of God's favor!"

In this petrol station, I started to praise God, and I discovered that it could be the most marvelous place on earth if I invited God. It was here that I started to write my book, *"Chased by Your Grace."*

I understood this day that God is…

A God of relationships.

From the first chapter of Genesis and all through the Bible, we can see that the Lord is a God of relationships, and relationships are at the heart of God's projects. Here are a few verses from Gen: 2.

Verse 18: *"The Lord God said, 'It is not good for the man to be alone. I will make a companion for him who corresponds to him.'"*. God sees that man cannot live alone. In fact, man seems to have similar needs to those of his Creator.

God, needing relationships himself, gives to Adam a woman who resembles him, and is of the same nature as him. The first institution is put in place to govern human relationships: marriage *"That is why a man leaves his father and mother and unites with his wife, and they become a new family."* Verse 24.

But God also created man to respond to his personal need for relationships. That is why God created man in his own image, to have this similarity with another, who resembles him. During the first chapters of Genesis, we see him visiting Adam and Eve daily. He comes to visit the first couple and is an integral part of their lives.

Alas, the first of an unending list of sins soon happens. We all know the spiritual consequences which lead from this fall: Romans 6: 23 *"For the payoff of sin is death, but the gift of God is eternal life in Christ Jesus our Lord."* Even though Adam and Eve don't die physically, they did enter a realm of death in that the immediate consequence is the shattering of both the human relationships and their relationship with God.

First of all, there is fear. Verse 10: *"The man replied, 'I heard you moving about in the orchard, and I was afraid because I was naked, so I hid.'"* The man feels fear and shame. It is interesting to point out that this will lead to the first death since the creation and the first sacrifice—the animal that God kills to use the skin to cover Adam and Eve's nudity and their shame.

Then comes the accusation, which always follows closely behind fear! Adam, after declaring that the woman is flesh of his flesh and bone of his bones, turns away from her and accuses her, verse 12: *"The man said, 'The woman whom you gave me, she gave me some fruit from the tree and I ate it.'"*.

Or to put it another way, it is the woman's fault. Not my wife, flesh of my flesh, but the woman whom YOU gave me. It's not my fault; it's everybody else's. From this day onward, human relationships became poisoned, a first fratricide happens, then wars, murders, genocide, abortion, suicide, etc.

Most of these things today are still caused by fears. The fear of others, of being left out, of being in want or need. How many of our relationships are tinged by our fears, even with those we love the most. *"But perfect love drives out fear!"*

Having acquired the knowledge of good and evil, humanity can only be terrorized by seeing God's holiness that humans can no longer share. The relationship with God is perverted by pride, and God cannot accept Cain's sacrifice—Cain, instead of accepting God's loving recommendations, throws himself into sin by rebelling by assassinating his brother.

From that moment on, the feelings of fear and pride will forever be at the heart of our relationships, with other people and with God.

But God has a plan that will re-establish this relationship. He throws a bridge over the void that Satan has dug between Him and humanity. This is a cross-shaped bridge, where at Calvary Jesus gave up his life so that we could be reconciled to the Father, and to others. This is how we have eternal life. Romans 5:10 *"For if while we were enemies we were reconciled to God through the death of his Son, how much more, since we have been reconciled, will we be saved by his life?"*

From this reconciliation flows the key to the authority that we have available to us when we are saved. This is part of our new identity.

Whom do you say I am?

You may know this passage from the gospel where Jesus asks this question to his disciples. Matthew 16:13–16: *"When Jesus came to the area of Caesarea Philippi, he asked his disciples, "Who do people say that the Son of Man is?" They answered, "Some say John the Baptist, other Elijah, and other Jeremiah or one of the prophets." He said to them, "But who do you say that I am?" Simon Peter answered, "You are the Christ, the Son of the living God."*

Jesus certainly didn't have an identity problem in asking confirmation from his disciples. However, the fact that they received and understood Jesus Identity was crucial for them to enter in their future calling.

It was just after this revelation that he told them about the plan of salvation: verses 18 & 21 *"And Jesus answered him, "You are blessed, Simon's son of Jonah, because flesh and blood did not reveal this to you, but my Father in heaven! And I tell you that you are Peter, and on this rock (Peter's declaration of Jesus's identity) I will build my church, and the gates of Hades will not overpower it… From that time on Jesus began to show his disciples that he must go to Jerusalem and suffer many things at the hands of the elders, chief priests, and experts in the law, and be killed, and on the third day be raised.'*

If the devil had convinced the religious leaders of the time to kill just a "prophet," no salvation would have been given. How many of God's prophets had already been killed? Matthew 23: 31: *"By saying this you testify against yourselves that you are descendants of those who murdered the prophets."*

Another dead prophet wouldn't change much. But killing the Son of God would change everything: This is the sacrificial Lamb!

In the beginning, even before conferring on him the power necessary to accomplish his ministry, God identifies Jesus. Matthew 3:16–17 *"After Jesus was baptized, just as he was coming up out of the water, the heavens opened and he saw the Spirit of God descending like a dove and coming on him. And a voice from heaven said, 'This is my one dear Son; in him I take great delight."*

It is important to realize that the sacrifice of Jesus only has value if He is the Son of God. To accept the fact he is a prophet, a man of God, even to accept his death *without realizing who he is*, God in the flesh is pointless!

It is interesting to note that when Satan came to tempt Jesus in the desert, he didn't question the power of the anointing that came down on him at the baptism, and made him a prophet, a high priest and a king. No,

Satan questioned Jesus's relationship to the father. Matthew 4; 3: *"The tempter came and said to him, 'If you are the Son of God, command these stones to become bread... If you are the Son of God, throw yourself down...".* And this lasted up until the last minute on the cross: Matt 27:40: *"If you are God's Son, come down from the cross!"!* But Jesus went to pass the identity test!

It is imperative to understand that if Jesus was not God's son, not only would the sacrifice be in vain, but all that he accomplished and his teaching would all be lies.

In fact, the desire of the devil is that we worship him instead of God. All his demons have the same desire, and pass themselves off as gods. Satan even tried to persuade the son of God himself to worship him: Matt 4; 8 to 10: *"Again, the devil took him to a very high mountain, and showed him all the kingdoms of the world and their grandeur. And he said to him, 'I will give you all these things if you throw yourself to the ground and worship me.' Then Jesus said to him, 'Go away, Satan! For it is written: "You are to worship the Lord your God and serve only him."""*.

We can see what happens when those who serve God find themselves worshipped:

Acts 14: 11 to 15: *"So when the crowds saw what Paul had done, they shouted in the Lycaonian language, "The gods have come down to us in human form!" They began to call Barnabas Zeus and Paul Hermes, because he was the chief speaker. The priest of the temple of Zeus, located just outside the city, brought bulls and garlands to the city gates; he and the crowds wanted to offer sacrifices to them. But when the apostles Barnabas and Paul heard about it, they tore their clothes and rushed out into the crowd, shouting, "Men, why are you doing these things? We too are men, with human natures just like you! We are proclaiming the good news to you, so that you should turn from these worthless things to the living God, who made the heaven, the earth, the sea, and everything that is in them."*

Revelation 7:10 *"So I threw myself down at his feet to worship him, but he said, 'Do not do this! I am only a fellow servant with you and your brothers who hold to the testimony about Jesus. Worship God, for the testimony about Jesus is the spirit of prophecy.'"*.

Revelation 22:9 *"But he said to me, 'Do not do this! I am a fellow servant with you and with your brothers the prophets, and with those who obey the words of this book. Worship God!'"*.

Jesus obviously knew the most important of the commandments. Luke 4: 8 *"'It is written, "You are to worship the Lord your God and serve only him."'"*. It is clear that if he had accepted for himself the worship of men, without being fully God, he would have placed himself in the devil's troops. Nothing would have been right!

But Jesus accepted worship from his disciples, without rebuking them:

Matt 2:11 *"As they came into the house and saw the child with Mary his mother, they bowed down and worshipped him. They opened their treasure boxes and gave him gifts of gold, frankincense, and myrrh."*

Matt 14: 33: *"Then those who were in the boat worshipped him, saying, 'Truly you are the Son of God.'"*.

Matt 28:17 *"When they saw him, they worshipped him."*

God would never have let someone take his identity and receive worship that is due to Him, without reacting! It is obvious that Jesus is legitimately allowed to be worshipped because of his identity.

He is God, in man's form, who died for our sins, and that means that today we can call out:

Abba, Father!

Lots of Christians have a hazy view of who they are in Christ. And how we see ourselves is what our everyday life depends on.

I have often been confronted by lean times, living as I do by faith. I often asked myself, how am I going to feed my family, give them a roof, take care of them, etc...

This also affected the disciples, and Jesus told them not to worry. He taught them in Luke 11:11–13: *"What father among you, if your son asks for a fish, will give him a snake instead of a fish? Or if he asks for an egg, will give him a scorpion?*

If you then, although you are evil, know how to give good gifts to your children, how much more will the heavenly Father give the Holy Spirit to those who ask him!"

I used to think why does Jesus put the emphasis on the Holy Spirit, as being the main gift that God wanted to give to his children, as a human father would give food to his brood?

The reason for this is that the promised Holy Spirit

is the only one to give us the certitude of our identity as children of God. Rom 8 : 14-16

« For all who are led by the Spirit of God are the sons of God. For you did not receive the spirit of slavery leading again to fear, but you received the Spirit of adoption, by whom we cry, 'Abba, Father.' The Spirit himself bears witness to our spirit that we are God's children ».

The blessing of God, our authority, the capacity to work miracles doesn't depend on what we do, but on WHO we are. We are co-inheritors with Christ because Christ's father has adopted us!

When a child is adopted, he changes identity to take on that of his new parents. On paper, he becomes the son of the person adopting him. His past is erased and his future is written in his new identity. Did you know that, legally, an adopted child has exactly the same rights and duties as a child who is born biologically of his parents? His part of the inheritance is the same.

Another thing, this lineage cannot be broken by the adoptive parents. Only the child has the right to break this "contract," under certain conditions.

This is exactly what happens when we are born again!

We become a full heir, with full inheritance with Christ, by the law of adoption of the Holy Spirit when we are born again! Not only do we receive the nations, to the ends of the earth, Ps 2:7–8: *"The king says, "I will announce the Lord's decree. He said to me: 'You are my so!*

This very day I have become your father! Ask me, and I will give you the nations as your inheritance, the ends of the earth as your personal property.' But God also gives us authority that goes with this inheritance.

Luke, 10 :17- 20: *'Then the seventy-two returned with joy, saying,'Lord, even the demons submit to us in your name!' So, he said to them, 'I saw Satan fall like lightning from heaven. Look, I have given you authority to tread on snakes and scorpions and on the full force of the enemy, and nothing will hurt you. Nevertheless, do not rejoice that the spirits submit to you, but rejoice that your names stand written in heaven.'".*

As I explained in my earlier book, *"Chased by Your Grace!"* this right is given to us from the foundation of the world. God has programed nobody for hell; this proves the love God has for us.

He wants no one to be lost: 1 Tim 2: 3 and 4 *"Such prayer for all is good and welcomed before God our Savior, since he wants all people to be saved and to come to the knowledge of the truth."* He had provided, even before the fall, for a way out by his grace.

Revelation 13:8 *"And all those who live on the earth will worship the beast, everyone whose name has not been written since the foundation of the world in the book of life belonging to the Lamb who was killed."*

The act of adoption was written, we just needed to sign it.

We have received a birth right, all of us on the

earth, and for all generations.

Birth rights!

The parable of the prodigal son. Luke 15:

"Then Jesus said, 'A man had two sons. The younger of them said to his father, "Father, give me the share of the estate that will belong to me." So he divided his assets between them. After a few days, the youngest son gathered together all he had and left on a journey to a distant country, and there he squandered his wealth with a wild lifestyle. Then after he had spent everything, a severe famine took place in that country, and he began to be in need. So he went and worked for one of the citizens of that country, who sent him to his fields to feed pigs. He was longing to eat the carob pods the pigs were eating, but no one gave him anything. But when he came to his senses he said, "How many of my father's hired workers have enough food to spare, but here I am dying from hunger! I will get up and go to my father and say to him, 'Father, I have sinned against heaven and against you. I am no longer worthy to be called your son; treat me like one of your hired workers.' So, he got up and went to his father. But while he was still a long way from home his father saw him, and his heart went out to him; he ran and hugged his son and kissed him. Then his son said to him, 'Father, I have sinned against heaven and against you; I am no longer worthy to be called your son.' But the father said to his slaves, 'Hurry! Bring the best robe, and put it on him! Put a ring on his finger and sandals on his feet! Bring the fattened calf and kill it! Let us eat and celebrate, because this son of mine was dead, and is alive

again he was lost and is found! So, they began to celebrate."

It is wonderful to see what God gave is in Jesus Christ. How many times have I read this story, and it has always moved me greatly.

Knowing that despite our errors, we have the possibility of coming back to God, who is always ready to forgive us, to welcome us, to wash our sins away … and to restore to us our identity.

Let's look at the story together.

Verses 17 to 19 *"But when he came to his senses he said, 'How many of my father's hired workers have enough food to spare, but here I am dying from hunger! I will get up and go to my father and say to him, "Father, I have sinned against heaven and against you. I am no longer worthy to be called your son; treat me like one of your hired workers. ""*.

Here is a son who wants to do things properly, he thinks it is right for him to return to his father, he realizes his mistake and repents of it. However, aware of the gravity of the situation, he thinks he is disqualified once and for all as son. He is having a crisis of identity. *"I am no longer worthy to be called your son; treat me like one of your hired workers."*

But the father doesn't wish to leave his son that way! *"Bring the best robe, and put it on him! Put a ring on his finger and sandals on his feet! Bring the fattened calf and kill it! Let us eat and celebrate, because this son of mine was dead, and is alive again—he was lost and is found!"*

One detail had escaped me until recently; the ring that the father puts on his son's finger. While watching the film "BEN HUR," a few years ago, I realized the value of the detail in the parable.

You will remember, if you have seen the film, that Ben HUR, having been adopted by a Roman captain, returns to Jerusalem and comes before the palace of the Roman governor. To enter into the palace, he uses his new identity, showing the Roman guard the ring "the seal" he was given, and his Roman identity is proven! What a surprise for his ex-best friend, become his worst enemy, when he realizes that he whom he thought dead is alive and full of a new authority conferred by his adoption!

As a result of seeing this, I did some historical research and found out that the family ring, or seal, was at that time a recognized proof of identity. Is this why Jesus said in this parable: "*Put a ring on his finger?*"

This precision in the text means that it is something important. The Father doesn't just clothes him and put shoes on him ... important things, of course, seeing what the son has been through. He also gives him back the family ring, proof of his identity, and all that this implies—the authority as a son in the house of his father!

Recall what the son says when he is in the pit of despair: *"I am no longer worthy to be called your son; treat me like one of your hired workers."* I am sure that he thought himself to be very spiritual. There is a human notion of justice, which places limits on the father's forgiveness; even if he comes home, he can no longer hope to be considered worthy of confidence in his father's eyes. But the fact is we are not called to be servants, but sons. The father doesn't hold with our identity crises!

In Rom 8: 15, it does not say that we have been hired by God, but that we have been adopted by God: *"For you did not receive the spirit of slavery leading again to fear, but you received the Spirit of adoption, by whom we cry, Abba, Father!"*

A good understanding of this fact is of prime importance if we want to fully enter into the prerogatives of children of God. Our authority in the house of our Father is conditioned by the fact that we are His children, so we must be fully aware of it.

Today God is not looking for more servants; he already has the angels, and all of creation to do that. What he wants is to get his children back! From Genesis through to Revelation, the Bible tells of a father who wants to find his lost children!

Even if we are called to serve God, He considers us much more than just slaves. Jesus declares in John 3:15,

"I no longer call you slaves, because the slave does not understand what his master is doing. But I have called you friends, because I have revealed to you everything I heard from my Fathe." We are sons who serve. Sons are who we are, serving is what we do.

Like all of God's promises in the Bible, until we grasp it, it will stay just as potential! In order to prevent us from entering into our true identity, Satan has been lying to us about our identity. We call this Identity Theft! So, ask him:

Who do you believe I am?

One of the devil's favorite ploys is to deny this adoption and therefore the authority that goes with it as a child of God. He did it with Jesus, we have already seen, in Matt 4: "*If you are the Son of God,*" and he will try with us, too. This is the Identity Test we must all go through.

As we have been so long separated from God, Satan generally starts with a bad image of the Father, either through our own fathers, or through our Judeo-Christian culture with its idea of a distant, cold God.

This strategy is as old as the hills. Throughout history when one civilization annihilated another, the generations were always broken, by separating children from their parents in order to cut them from their roots. The story of Daniel and his companions is an obvious example.

We can see how the devil attacks the family unit, and has been doing so for centuries. This results in entire generations who lose their roots, lose their identity.

I was watching the movie "Merry Christmas" which was about the fraternization at Christmas 1917 between enemy camps in the trenches of the First World War, and I realized that this butchery was in line with this strategy. Not a single family in France, Germany or Britain was untouched, at least one death in every household. How many children had their identity and lineage thus stolen? God certainly had great plans for this generation, who saw technical inventions come to be, and the possibility of seeing all of creation touched by the gospel.

This rupture is also found in the church, where adult Christians are formed instead of Christian parents, full of unconditional love for their spiritual children.

If we disconnect from the Father, we only have our fleshly identity left. This causes so many problems, even after years of being a Christian. This is why we absolutely need to...

Did we ever meet him?

Acts 9:1–7: *"During those days, Saul, full of angry threats and rage, wanted to murder the disciples of the Lord Jesus. So, he went to ask the high priest and requested a letter of authorization he could take to the Jewish leaders in Damascus, requesting their cooperation in finding and arresting any who were followers of the Way. Saul wanted to capture all of the believers he found, both men and women, and drag them as prisoners back to Jerusalem. So, he obtained the authorization and left for Damascus. Just outside the city, a brilliant light flashing from heaven suddenly exploded all around him. Falling to the ground, he heard a booming voice say to him, "Saul, Saul, why are you persecuting me?" The men accompanying Saul were stunned and speechless, for they heard a heavenly voice but could see no one. Saul replied, "Who are you, Lord?"*

"I am Jesus, the Victorious, the one you are persecuting. Now, get up and go into the city, where you will be told what you are to do."

We have all heard of this wonderful conversion of Saul of Tarsus who became the Apostle Paul and to whom we owe two thirds of the New Testament.

In rereading this text, we can ask ourselves the following question: How this man, Saul of Tarsus, member of the pharisees' party who certainly had the greatest knowledge of the Scriptures at that time, who was Jewish, who had lived in Jerusalem and studied with a great teacher of the time, Gamaliel, who was full of zeal and fire for God... How this man can ask this question: WHO ARE YOU, LORD?

The answer seems clear to me! Saul studied God a lot, but never met him!

It's possible to study Chopin's life, his work, his psychological portrait, his culture ... but if I ask you the question: "did you met him," you will necessarily say no! Chopin died long before you or your parents or grandparents were born. If you were ever meeting Chopin in a party, you wouldn't recognize him!
Just as Saul was unable to recognize Christ when he met him on the road to Damascus!

We can recognize only whom we have already met and only those who are contemporary with us, who are alive at the same time as us. For the others, we can only study their lives or their works.

I like to study the lives of the characters in the Bible, especially those heroes of the faith who were David, Daniel, Paul...
But I have no chance to meet them, because they are dead.
But I know I can, and I have to meet Jesus, because He's alive!

Too many people today are willing to study the life of Jesus, some even seek to apply with all their hearts his teachings. They preached and lectured about him, studied his every word, probed ancient history in search of evidence of his life and work, but they never met him. Theology universities are full of these people. A friend of mine in the United States had his Doctorate of Theology years before meeting Jesus and entering ministry.

We can read in Matthew's gospel the story of those people who tell Christ: *"Not everyone who calls out to me, "Lord! Lord!" will enter the Kingdom of Heaven. Only those who actually do the will of my Father in heaven will enter. On judgment day, many will say to me, "Lord! Lord! We prophesied in your name and cast out demons in your name and performed many miracles in your name." But I will reply, "I never knew you. Get away from me, you who break God's laws.'* (Matt 7:22–23)

We need to understand that Jesus is less interested in you performing miracles than in "knowing you."

Let us take up the case of our "friend" Chopin. Today, many people play Chopin on their piano, it is one of the most studied composers in learning this instrument, I myself can hum some of its tunes.

That doesn't make me Chopin's friend!

Remember that story in Acts 19:13–16: *"A group of Jews was traveling from town to town casting out evil spirits. They tried to use the name of the Lord Jesus in their incantation, saying, 'I command you in the name of Jesus, whom Paul preaches, to come out!' Seven sons of Sceva, a leading priest, were doing this. But once when they tried it, the evil spirit replied, 'I know Jesus, and I know Paul, but who are you?' Then the man with the evil spirit leaped on them, overpowered them, and attacked them with such violence that they fled from the house, naked and battered."*

These people had heard of a certain Jesus, and knew that a certain Paul was preaching in his name. They had also learned that Paul's preaching was accompanied by extraordinary signs and wonders, including that of casting out demons. Then they thought that this power could serve their profession of exorcism. So, they tried to reproduce Paul's technic but they did not know Paul and did not know Jesus! So, there could be nothing in their hearts but greed, selfishness, pride, for they had not known the one who changes hearts!

We see how it ended for them! Oh, they knew the law, they had studied it with their father, one of the chief priests. They had even studied God … but never knew him!

We must realize what the verb "to know" used by Christ means. It is the same term used in the Bible to express the intimate relationship between a married man and a woman. For example: "Adam knew Eve, his wife; she conceived, and bore Cain." This notion shows us that this concept of knowing implies absolute intimacy. When we know someone, in the biblical sense of the term, we become one with him or her. Ephesians 5:31 *"A man leaves his father and mother and is joined to his wife, and the two are united into one."*

When we know Christ, we are supposed to become one flesh with Him. Which implies that we become the imprint of who he is. It's supposed to be as if we are a mirror reflecting his glory. People must be able to discern Christ in us. Jesus said that he knew the Father and that whoever saw him saw the Father.

Let's read together this revealing passage on this subject in John 14: "*Jesus said to him: 'I am the way, the truth, and the life. No one comes to the Father except through me. If you knew me, you would also know my Father. And now you know him, and you've seen him.' Philip said to him: 'Lord, show us the Father, and that is enough for us. Jesus said to him: "I have been with you so long, and you have not known me, Philip! He who has seen me has seen the Father; how do you say, show us the Father? Do you not believe that I am in the Father, and that the Father is in me? The words that I say to you, I do not say of myself; and the Father who dwells in me, it is he who does the works."*

We understand, reading that scripture, the absolute intimacy that exists between the Son and the Father. When we see one, we discover the other. This unity between the Father and the Son, Jesus prays that it may also be the sharing of His disciples with Him! *I am no longer in the world, and they are in the world, and I go to you. Holy Father, keep them in your name which you have given me, that they may be one like us.*' Being ONE with the Son makes us participants in His power, '*they will do the same things as I and even the greatest…*' but also participants in His glory to come, 1 Peter 5:1.

This would certainly make us happy to be able to stop there, but we are also called to be participants in its rejection!

'I gave them your word; and the world hated them, because they are not of the world, as I am not of the world.

We theoretically recognize those who have known Christ because they manifest His person in the world. When the disciples in Antioch were given the nickname "Christian," it was out of mockery. They were called little Christ! I wish people would make fun of us because they recognized us as a little Christ! Unfortunately, this is rarely the case.

Nowadays, it is difficult to tell the difference at first sight between those who serve Christ and those who do not. Of course, we find here and there a "fish bumper sticker" on a car, but this never made anyone look like Christ!

The truth is that we often hesitate to be recognized. We are the "very secret" agents in Her Majesty's service. Mikaël BOND 007! I'm on a secret mission ... discretion ... discreetly discreet mission...

This never was God's plan for us to be that discreet. God's plan is for you to go against this world and turn it upside down.

We want to sanctify ourselves ... but discreetly. We

don't want people to know. It's like the story so common of the young Christian who in high school comes at the cost of great efforts to resist the devil. He keeps himself pure and has chosen not to let himself get flirtatious. Often, with God's grace, he succeeds. But when his classmates ask him if he's ever been out with a girl, he says yes, of course! It would shock my friends if they found out that I go to church, that I want to remain a virgin until marriage! he doesn't want to look like too weird!

Do you not believe that Jesus shocked the people of his generation? If we have known Christ, we should become like him and we would necessarily shock people.

The Bible tells us that the Gospel is madness for this world! 1 Corinthians 1:18 *"For the preaching of the cross is foolishness to those who perish."*

"Shocking no one" is Satan's best weapon! Today, every time I hear in my heart the little phrase: "Take it easy on the Gospel, be careful not to shock," I know where it comes from!

Be awarded, I'm not telling you to shock just for the sake to shock. Our role is above all to love people. Some people just like to shock for the fun of seeing people shocked. They become stumbling blocks!

But we must know that we cannot avoid shocking people if we want the gospel to be preached and those same people to be saved. What do you prefer, not to shock people and let them go quietly to hell?

In reality, our problem comes from the fact that we are afraid of being rejected. The fear of rejection makes Christians today less and less like Christ.

We do not hesitate to shock certain people with our outfit, with our language… We are often provoking when it comes to asserting our identity! Especially if it allows us to integrate a group of people we have chosen. Our desire not to shock is in fact only an excuse not to be ejected out of the social group in which we want to find a place. The idea of exclusion is simply unbearable!

Yet we should expect this if we have known Christ, for He warned us from the beginning in this verse of John 16:2–3: *"They will exclude you from the synagogues; and even the hour is coming when whoever kills you will believe he is worshipping God. And they will do so, because they have known neither the Father nor I."*

When we have known the Lord, we want to remain in Him and He in us, so we begin to look more look Him. This implies that we sanctify ourselves by His grace, more and more, and that we implement our salvation in a concrete way.

We will therefore follow his commandments, which for those who do not follow them quickly becomes unbearable.1 John 2:3 *"If we keep his commandments, we know by this that we knew him."*

How many times have I seen old friends turn away from me because I didn't want to do drugs, drink, steal? I saw others turn away from me, sometimes even within my family, because I had decided to love, as Christ commanded us, a neighbor whom they considered unlovable. You choose, it's him or us!

People who were close to me became strangers because of my desire to be Christ like, because this resemblance confronted them with their sins and echoed their conscience which also accused them.

Ever since he tasted the tree of knowledge of good and evil, man has tried to forget it. He wants to silence his conscience, but it wakes up every time it is confronted by the manifestation of Christ's grace!

This is what shocks people: God gives grace, while their knowledge of good and evil accuses them. They can't bear to see you free of these accusations while they remain slaves to them!

Having known grace is the only way to walk free from sin. Colossians 1:6 *"This same Good News that came to you is going out all over the world. It is bearing fruit everywhere by changing lives, just as it changed your lives from the day you first heard and understood the truth about God's wonderful grace."*

This is the only way to really be "little Christ," we need to live this intimacy with God's grace if we want to be free! It is not enough to understand the mechanism of grace, we must immerse ourselves in it

… from the day you heard and knew the grace of God.'

We find in the Old Testament the word grace which in Hebrew is said: 'kheh'-sed' and is translated in the Bible by kindness, mercy, fidelity, love, grace…

Grace, as we see, is the very nature of God. We must therefore learn to know intimately the nature of God, and we will be able to say that we are known by Him.

Rediscover our true identity!

Ephesians 4:20–24

*'But you did not learn about Christ like this, if indeed you heard about him and were taught in him, just as the truth is in Jesus. You were taught with reference to your former way of life to lay aside the old man who is being corrupted in accordance with deceitful desires, to be renewed in the spirit of your mind, and to put on the new man who has been created in God's image—**in righteousness and holiness that comes from truth**.'*

We can see that beyond our body and human nature there is a spiritual person: our new nature. This is the new man, who is the inheritor of eternal life, and has authority from his adoption.

2 Corinthians 5:17 *'So then, if anyone is **in (living relationship with)** Christ, he is a new creation; what is old has passed away—look, what is new has come!'*

It is this 'new man' we need to consider, first of all, if we want to be efficient/healthy Christians in God's kingdom.

Rom 12:2 *"Do not be conformed to this present world, but be transformed by the renewing of your mind, so that* *you may test and approve what is the will of God—what is good and well-pleasing and perfect"*.

It is impossible for us, not only to please God, but also to enter into our destiny with actions produced by the old nature! We can teach the 'old man' to sing Christian songs, to speak 'in tongues,' to pray in an evangelical way, but none of these are spiritual. Our flesh can only produce fleshy things!

What pleases God, and what he seeks above all else, is a quality relationship with his children, acquired only through Jesus on the cross. All the rest is just religion.

Who are we today?

Christ is the Head! We are the body!
The demons are under Jesus" feet. Therefore, they are under our feet, too! ALLELUIA!

The Messiah is crowned, he reigns, at the right hand of God, but his authority rests on his shoulders *"For a child has been born to us, a son has been given to us and the government will be on his shoulders"* Isaiah 9.6.7.
The shoulders are not part of the head, they are part of the body. It is on the body of Christ, which is the church that the government rests. The Hebrew term "misrah," signifies authority, the government!

The aim of the devil is to place burdens on our shoulders, which tie us down, so we cannot exercise our authority: Matt.23.4. *"They tie up heavy loads, hard to carry, and put them on men's shoulders, but they themselves are not willing even to lift a finger to move them."*

Satan is more aware of who we are than we are ourselves! He knows that as sons and daughters of the Most High, we have a legitimate authority over all of our heavenly father's possessions: Matt 6:18 *"I tell you the truth, whatever you bind on earth will have been bound in heaven, and whatever you release on earth will have been released in heaven."*

This authority is there to put into place the decrees of the Kingdom.

The Bible says in Colossians 1:18: *"He is the head of the body, the church."*
The day that I realized that even if I was only a bit of hard skin on Jesus' feet, my position was still higher than that of the devil and demons, I knew that I could walk to victory!

Christ is in the heavens, at the right hand of God, and he has trusted us to establish the kingdom government, and to exercise authority in his name, because we have the same divine lineage
as him!

God has reconciled us to himself in Jesus Christ. But now we need to be reconciled with ourselves to live a blossoming Christian life.

Luke 10:27 *"The expert answered, 'Love the Lord your God with all your heart, with all your soul, with all your strength, and with all your mind, and love your neighbor as yourself."*

We have to understand that we cannot love our neighbor until we haven't learned to love ourselves, and this means being reconciled with our own identity.

Get off your failures!

"Late one afternoon, after his midday rest, David got out of bed and was walking on the roof of the palace. As he looked out over the city, he noticed a woman of unusual beauty taking a bath. He sent someone to find out who she was, and he was told, 'She is Bathsheba, the daughter of Eliam and the wife of Uriah the Hittite.'… Then David sent messengers to get her; and when she came to the palace, he slept with her became pregnant. She warns David.

David immediately addressed the following order to General Joab: Send me Uri the Hittite… David says to him: go home and get some rest. Uri left the palace but Uri did not go to his house… The next morning David wrote a letter to Joab and entrusted it to Uri. He said: place Uri on the front line, where the fight is most violent, then withdraw leaving him alone, so that he may be hit by the enemy and die.

When Uriah's wife heard that her husband was dead, she mourned for him. When the period of mourning was over, David sent for her and brought her to the palace, and she became one of his wives… But the Lord was displeased with what David had done. He sent the prophet Nathan to

David... And this is what the Lord, the God of Israel, says: Why, then, have you despised the word of the Lord and done this horrible deed? ...

Then David confessed to Nathan, 'I have sinned against the Lord.' Nathan replied, 'Yes, the Lord has forgiven you, and you won't die for this sin. Nevertheless, because you have shown utter contempt for the word of the Lord by doing this, your child will die.'

David begged God to spare the child. He went without food and lay all night on the bare ground. After a week, the child died.

Then David got up from the ground, washed himself, put on lotions, and changed his clothes. He went to the Tabernacle and worshiped the Lord. After that, he returned to the palace and was served food and ate. Then David comforted Bathsheba, his wife, and slept with her. She became pregnant and gave birth to a son, and David named him Solomon. The Lord loved the child and sent word through Nathan the prophet that they should name him Jedidiah which means 'beloved of the Lord,' as the Lord had commanded!" From Samuel's second book

I am sure that like me you already know the story of David and Bathsheba, and I am sure that like me, you wondered how a man according to the heart of God, who was the greatest king of Israel, could have fallen into such a sordid story.

Any court would have sentenced David to death or at least life sentence! Maybe not for his adultery, but for the premeditated murder he ordered on Uri!

But not only did God give him grace, but He will

also bless David and Bathsheba and their offspring since this one appears in the genealogy of Christ! (Matthew 1.)

In fact, what God teaches us through this story and what seems important to receive from this is not the sin itself, but the way David gets up from that fall!

A child of God is not a person who never falls, in no case someone perfect. A true child of God is measured by his ability to get up after his failures!

When the devil tempts you, and tries to make you fall, his goal is not "sin" for itself! He knows very well that all past and future sins are washed away in the blood of Jesus for him who believes in the grace granted by the Messiah to the cross! No, his purpose is different! He's only looking for one thing: he wants to stop you in your walk to the call that God has placed upon your life!

God does not repent of the call He has placed on David's life, and many of us should think twice before condemning God's servants who fall. Let us not forget that we will be judged with the same measure that we use to judge others!

If God does not renounce His call, why should we refuse those who have fallen to stand up and return to their service?

Then, for the one who has fallen, it is so important that he consider the thing from a constructive angle, so, he does not add the desertion of God's plan to the first failure.

What would have become of Israel if its Hero Joshua had turned back because of his defeat before the city of Ai? (Joshua 7) or if David the great King, covered in guilt, had let himself go into depression and had abandoned the throne? (2 Samuel 11) If Elijah, after having defeated the prophets of BAAL, and then after having fled into the wilderness before Jezebel, had not started again? (1 Kings 19) If Peter, after his half-failed water walk, had returned home to take over his fishing business? (Matthew 14) If Paul, before the questions of the Jew and the questioning of his apostolate had decided to open a Kosher restaurant. (1 Corinthians 9).

All these people had failures and all got up again! Don't let the devil win! It will happen only if you refuse to stand up again after you fall!

May the Lord bless you in your new identity in Christ, may His Grace lead you to discover a little more of it each day.

Best regards, Mikaël REALE

Table of contents

Where have you been, Son?	7
A God of relationships.	13
Whom do you say I am?	16
Abba, Father!	21
Birth rights!	25
Who do you believe I am?	29
Did we ever meet him?	31
Rediscover our true identity!	41
Who are we today?	43
Get off your failures!	45

Another title by Mikaël REALE

Chase by your Grace.

Follow him on Facebook: Mikael REALE